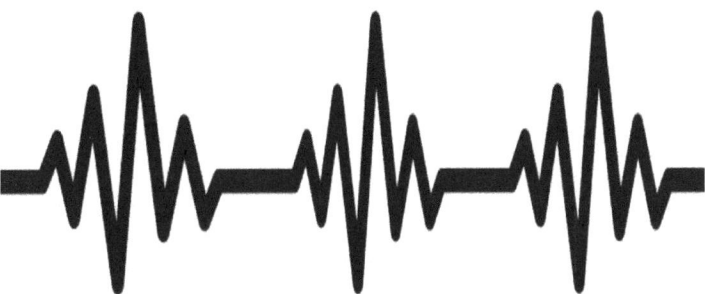

THE HUMAN CONDITION IS A TERMINAL ILLNESS

MATTHEW J. HALL

BareBackPress

This is a work of fiction. The characters, incidents, and dialogue are the products of the author's imagination and are not to be construed as real. Any resemblance to actual events or person, living or dead, is entirely coincidental.

BareBackPress
Hamilton, Ontario, Canada
For enquiries visit www.barebackpress.com
Cover photo, layout and design by Peter Jelen

No part of this can be used or reproduced in any manner whatsoever without written permission, except in the case of brief quotations embodied in critical articles and reviews. For information address BareBackPress.

COPYRIGHT © 2017 Matthew J. Hall
All RIGHTS RESERVED
ISBN-13: 978-1926449111
ISBN-10:1926449118

PETROL STATION - 1
SMILE THIEF - 10
BLUER SHADE OF GREEN - 12
HELLION - 13
STICKS LIKE STUBBORN PLASTIC - 16
GUTLESS - 17
THE BEST I COULD DO - 18
GETTING CREATIVE - 19
FALLING IN LOVE WITH A PHOTOGRAPH - 20
EVEN MY DAYDREAMS ARE DAMNED - 21
THE DAY'S HOPELESS PATTERNS - 22
MAKE ME THINK TWICE - 23
THE BIRDS WERE YET TO START SINGING - 24
LOVE SEAT - 26
FUCKING NIEGHBOURS - 27
BIG CLEAR TEAR - 28
TRESPASSING - 29
HER LAST LETTER - 30
I'D LIKE TO HAND THIS NIGHT OVER - 31
THEIR SADNESS AND MINE - 32
IT CAN WAIT - 33
TAKING BACK TIME - 34
SOMETIMES YOU MEET SOMEONE - 35
IF I WERE AN ARTIST - 36
PORTRAIT - 37
MAGNOLIA - 38
HER SHADOWS AND MINE - 39
TRUTH WHISPERS - 40
FRENCH MANICURE - 41
YESTERDAY'S NEWS - 42

SEASIDE - 43
GHOST WOMAN - 45
AN UNDER BITE AND ADDITIONAL NEEDS - 46
WILLIAM HILL - 47
AN OLD SONG - 48
DEATH ON A SUNDAY AFTERNOON - 51
THE GRAPEFRUIT IS NOT A METAPHOR - 52
THREE LITTLE PIGGIES - 53
WAR CRY - 54
YOU ARE A ONETIME DEAL - 55
QUICK AND FAST - 57
BIRD ON BLACK WATER - 58
MOTHS DRESSED AS BUTTERFLIES - 59
CRUELER THAN KIDS - 61
PREDESTINATION - 64
FAITH - 65
IN HER LETTERS 66
SOME DAYS - 68
IT'S ALL LIES - 69
IT'S COMPLICATED - 70
TEA FOR TWO - 71
A MUSIC THEORY - 72
ANOTHER LIFE, ANOTHER WORLD - 73
ALWAYS FIGHTING - 75
CONFESSIONS - 77
INCARCERATED IN CANVAS - 78
TRAPPED INSIDE MY FURNITURE - 79
PATTI'S STILL GOT IT - 81
PLAY THE SAD VIOLIN - 84
DEAD STARS - 87
SADDEST SONG IN THE WORLD - 88
AS IF EVERYTHING WERE OKAY - 89
SINISTER TREE - 90
GOODNIGHT - 91

WHEN WE WERE KIDS - 92
EARLY GRAVE - 94
AS THE CROW FLIES - 95
TIME AND SPACE - 96
DEAD HOPE - 97
DOPPELGANGER - 98
MY MANNEQUIN AND I - 99
DRUNK ON YOUR TEARS - 100
THE WOMAN WHO ALLOWED HIM LOVE - 101
FADE AWAY - 102
HE LEFT HIS SOUL ON THE FLOOR - 103

FOR
ESTHER MAY
THERE ARE NO WORDS

AND

MARCY ERB
MY FRIEND OF LETTERS

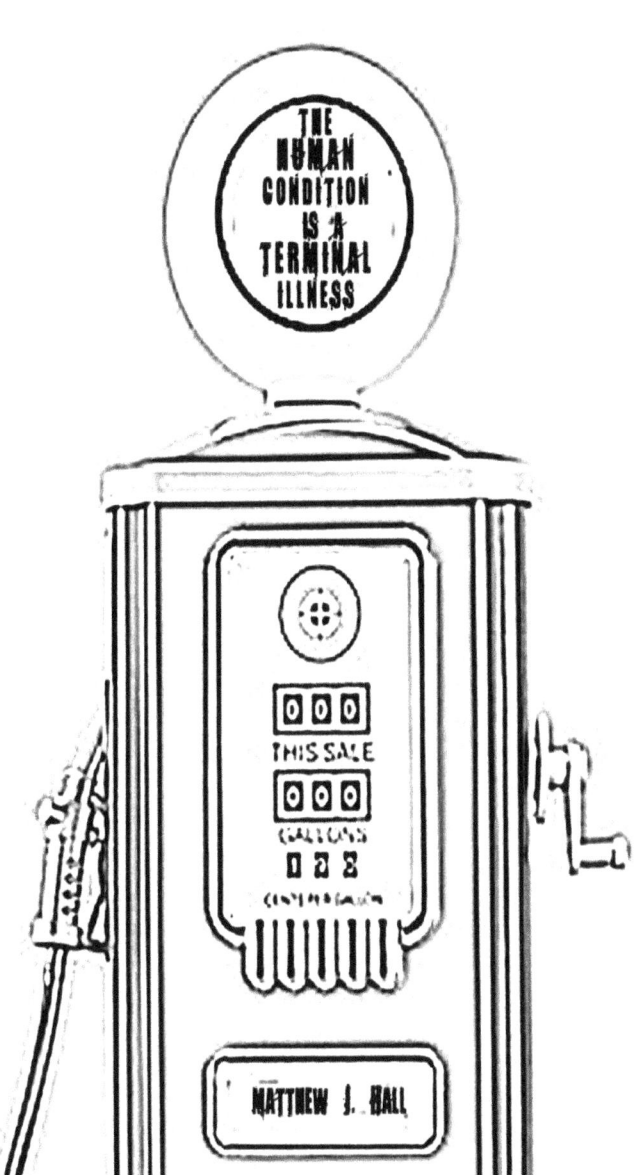

petrol station

I took a job at a petrol station
I needed a job
I'll stay for six months, I said

four years of ill-feeling later
I left

you'd think
a job like that
where time was measured
by all those thousands of interactions
that the poems would flow

but they didn't
they wouldn't
no matter how hard I tried

there were very few stories
in all those dead eyes
and seldom a poetic line
from all those loose mouths

there was nothing to say about the functional drunk
who fashioned a habit out of interrupting
my cigarette break
who'd lecture me on the unethical practice
of selling booze from a petrol station

it's the oil industry, mate
I'd say
as soon as we step foot on the forecourt
we're on morally shaky ground

he'd pretend not to hear me
and make a big production

out of paying for his generic vodka
with a credit card
which, without exception
never failed to decline

he'd reach inside his jacket
rummage around in there
pull out half-smoked cigarettes
betting slips
loose matches
a well-used handkerchief
and finally a five and change
all of which he'd put in a pile
and invite me to extract the necessary funds

I thought, perhaps the beggar
the one I slung a quid to on occasion
might do or say something of note

the one who came into the shop late one night
looked at the price of confectionary
called me a cunt
paid for a 75p bar of chocolate with a score
picked up his change with fussy fingers
muttering under his breath about,
this cunt's ripping me off

I thought I might get a poem or two
out of the school boy in uniform

a handsome young fellow
whose eyes bulged at the sugary treats
I was sure I'd get a page or two out of his greed
and how I related to it
something about the early stages of addiction
and the unfortunate path he had started on
but I was wrong

there was however
something to be said
about the chronic alcoholic
big old piss-patch on his trousers
and fear in his voice
a good man but easily distracted
kept threatening to bring on over a batch of his short stories
and read them to me, out loud, right there in the shop

and maybe
if I'm lucky
at some point
I'll get a few stanzas out of the chef
who always stank of spilt wine
yet never appeared drunk
he told me he couldn't cook for shit
but knew how to gamble and drink

there was always Cathy, though
she was an open book
from which I willfully stole
line after line
poem after poem

and some of those poems were picked up
by small-time publishers
placed in magazines
and a handful of people
read all about Cathy

they read about her true smile
and her rotten teeth
about her undeniable freedom
in spite of her obvious bounds

and the dirt on her eyelids

and her worn down heels
and the sadness of screaming failure
and her girlish innocence
of which she had no legitimate claim

and in other poems
which weren't picked up
they didn't read
about her fascination with fire
about the burns and soot-stained skin

they didn't read about the bruises
all over her neck
how she told me,
my friend grabbed me there
and tried to twist my head

nor did they read
about the time she told me,
I love you
she hadn't meant to say that

she'd come into the station
to tell me she didn't have any cigarettes
knowing full well I'd roll her one of my own
which I did
as she left, she said it, she said
I love you

all in a flush of red she retracted
I mean, I like you
I mean, you're a good man
I mean, thank you

I wanted to say
I know
but I just stood there

with dumb-grinning eyes
and watched her leave

the first time I met her
she approached the point of service
with two pockets of jingling change
she dug deep in there
and spilled all those one and two pence pieces
over the counter

I counted up the money
and swapped it for
a five pound note
a 50p
a 10p
and a 5p
and she smiled

and the smile cracked the grime on her face
from the corners of her thin mouth
all the way up to her deep crow's feet

when she left
the manager, with a smug sense of self, said
I have a theory about her
I think she's the local prostitute

any half-idiot could see
she was no type of scrubber
for sure, desperate times
demand desperate measures
and she may well have knelt down
given some head
but that didn't make her a part of the oldest profession

the manager, however
was a whole idiot

and couldn't see much of anything at all

a year or so later
at the end of a night shift
when the morning people
were fueling up
buying newspapers
cigarettes
sandwiches
coffee and the like

I stared out of the big glass window
and watched Cathy saunter up the street
she stopped at a bin and rifled through it
discarding the rubbish on the floor
at her feet

once she was satisfied
that the bin held nothing of worth
she picked up the litter she had dropped
and put it back into the bin

there was a delicacy to her movements
she was the crippled ballerina

a regular customer
nodded in Cathy's direction
crack head, he said
sorry? I said
she's a crack head, he said
oh, yeah, I said
adding,
it's ravished her body
but is yet to chew through her soul

the regular customer looked at me
as though I'd shit on the counter between us

paid for his coffee and got out

sometimes when walking to work
or walking home
or just walking the city with neither plan nor purpose
I would see Cathy asking people for change

and when she saw me
and saw that I'd seen her
she'd wave bashfully
and I could see she was ashamed
so I'd pretend not to have noticed her
and I'd walk the other way

Cathy was the only line of poetry
in that box of artificial light
built on a foundation of greed and illegal practice
there was nothing else to say

working at the petrol station
suicide was often on my mind
I was often bored
more often depressed
and more often than not,
disabled by a raging sense of anxiety

I realised early on
that the general public's common stupidity
was symptomatic of lots and lots of
individual selfishness
and their anxiety was contagious;
the human condition is a terminal illness

they were all in a rush
wanted to be first
wanted to win a fight that didn't exist

the factories and the warehouses
put me in good stead for the boredom
and depression is a waiting game
but anxiety is a wild and unpredictable beast

occasionally, customers would stand waiting
at an abandoned till
while I hid in the storeroom
with the Coca-Cola and crisps
and tried, with limited success
to stop crying

I longed for a fire
a big fuck-off forecourt explosion
or a gun-point robbery
or an honest-to-goodness lunatic
who'd tie me up in back
and subject me to prolonged acts of obscenity
anything other than the dead line of repeated routine

but I was a coward
stuck in a rut
too scared to move on
yet petrified of living out my days
activating pumps
and printing VAT receipts

I learnt
not too long ago
through a mutual acquaintance of ours
that they'd finally come along
and taken Cathy away

she's in the mad house
he said
she got herself a nice wee flat
he said

and she burnt it to the ground

what hospital is she in?
I asked
don't know and don't care
he answered

I could have easily found out
gone for a visit
taken her some cigarettes and flowers
seen about that true-smile of hers

but I didn't
and I won't
because I've left the petrol station
and I've exhausted its poems
so the next line
will have to come
from somewhere else

smile thief

I used to like watching Saturday cartoons
my feet dangling and bumping the sofa
the horrors of school, distant and far removed

then one such Saturday I broke my gaze
and searched the room for the voice I'd heard, demanding

and there was nobody
and the piano we all used to play sat idle
and the doorway held an empty space
and the emptiness was sickly and quiet

so who the hell had told me I had no right to smile?
I wiped that silly bastard from my face
and hid it under the cushions
deep inside the furniture on which I sat

years later I went back
grimly determined
hell-bent on finding it

I cut that cunt of a sofa
and tore out its fluff and flesh

but the cartoons didn't quite cut it
and the piano was well and truly out of tune
and the sadness bowed the door frame
and the taunting teachers
and the grief of it all
and the empty echoes of childish prayers
and the years of binging
and the fucking painkillers
and the heroin
and the booze
all looked back at me and laughed

I remember my last day of school
a buddy kept talking about
how we would remember each other for ever
I told him
I just want to forget

he seemed hurt
and he told me to fuck off

doubled over in that sofa
searching for my smile
and that demanding voice and my youth
I saw my friend and heard his rebuke
but my smile was nowhere to be seen

bluer shade of green

being prepubescent, we had no need for nervousness
we rolled freely on the bed
she had green eyes and smelt like clean clothes

I kissed her long, blonde hair and soft lips
I kissed her face repeatedly
her mouth touched my neck
her fingertips skimmed the tops of my ears

she was breath taking
and I think of her often
and I often think of the last time I saw her
sitting at the far side of her mother's oak table

she didn't seem to remember
her eyes seemed a bluer shade of green

in spite of everything suggesting otherwise
I touched her oak hidden foot with mine
she flinched, obviously perplexed

I pulled back as discretely as I had reached out
and we sat silently while our mothers talked

hellion

after school
on the school field
we got through
many bottles and cans
of white lightning
and special brew

sitting around
talking in small circles
alcoholic souls
in the bodies of boys

and once we were
good and drunk
we'd embark on a wild spree
of mindless vandalism

setting fires
spraying paint
and smashing glass

on one such occasion
I took a brick
and threw it through
one of the many panes
in Mr Mcgilligan's window

as the glass shattered
all over his office floor
I realised that every act of destruction
leading up to this act of destruction
had been an exercise in pointless petulance

I took another brick
and another

and another
and smashed every pane of glass

the following morning
in the clutches of a hangover
way beyond my years
I sat in Mr Mcgilligan's class

a sweat box of a room
hand-made platitudes
bordered the walls

DON'T FIX THE BLAME
FIX THE PROBLEM

and

YOU'RE ONLY AS SMALL
AS YOUR BIGGEST IDEA

and so on

looking at Mcgilligan's red face
I wondered if I might vomit
and he looked at mine
and rolled his beady eyes

"well," he demanded, jabbing a fat little finger
an inch from my face "what's the answer, boy?
If you don't know it by now then you never will!"

he steadied his hand
and the blur subsided
I searched for the answer
but didn't know what to say

I looked at his fat little finger

at all of his fat little fingers
and I saw lots of little cuts
from where he'd tidied up the shattered glass

and all in a breeze of clarity
my hangover left me
I felt good
and in the remembering
I feel good now
I realised I had known the answer all along
but I never did share it
with Mr Mcgilligan

sticks like stubborn plastic

I wanted to write like the tough old guy
I won't name him
you know who he is
our shelves are stuffed to sickness
with his books

all those volumes about
fucking and fighting
blood on the page
and all that tired old shit

I wrote several hundred poems
in this fashion
drinking my wine and whiskey
churning out vain lines
of stubborn plastic

a weak imitation
a tepid glass of water
a warm cup of death

I'm sober now
seldom reckless
know something about love and grace
and from time to time it comes through

the writing is still vain
but that's the way I like it
it's honest and its mine

gutless

I drew you a pencil picture
on the backside of a bus ticket
you were nestling into the underside of my left arm
we were old, had grown old together
the shading was shaky, but you would have seen
that we were sitting on our bench
at the foot-end of our tree
swift birds were overhead
a winding path and thick grass at our feet
my legs were crossed
I think it would have made you smile
but as I got off the bus
I tossed it in the used ticket box
because love is too dangerous
and I am a coward

the best I could do

I wanted to do something romantic for you
because in spite of the senseless circle
you have shown me sharp corners
where destination and journey merge
and a single moment becomes all of life
and all of life becomes whole

I wanted to say thank you
I wanted to do something romantic for you
I wanted to give you something special
I wanted to say something of your truth
wanted to find that honest line and lay it out at your feet

but the rose petals ripped under my ball-point pen
and the thorns on the spindly stem
were too small and obstinate
the poesy wouldn't fit no matter how tiny the words

so I pinned our poem to a homing bird's leg
whispered words of instruction and sent him off
but he had a mind of his own
he flew around and around and around as though he were lost
then he spotted some discarded food
and with our words he stopped

I wanted to do something romantic for you
and with regret
I am afraid
this, my love
is the best I could do

getting creative

incomplete images masquerading as dreams
danced on the inside of my eyelids
taunting my effort toward sleep and peace

I thought about the telephone
fingered the numbers
even picked up the receiver
imagined your voice and
finding my own

In truth, I knew you would turn me to soft clay
if I dialed, so I sculpted your bust
carefully
included your warts and
vindictive ways
gave extra attention to your eyes
made them brighter and slightly wider
I wanted you to see me
at last

when you were ready I explained
how I wanted to hurt you
how I wouldn't be sorry, at least not
in the traditional sense

several of the tight metallic bands were
loosened from my chest
as I kissed a soft farewell
on your drying cheek

when I was done I pummeled you
with a rolling pin
drank a glass of cold milk
sculpted something beautiful from your remains
climbed back into bed
and slept

falling in love with a photograph

I lived at the time alone in a three bedroom terraced house
each night I played guitar in front of the television
surrounded by photographs of people I once knew
when I went to bed late I looked at the photo of her on my bedside
it was the last and first thing I looked at every day
I thought about leaving the gas on and going to sleep
but knew there was little fairness in a move like that
every time I looked at that photograph she was smiling
and in the end I became tired of it
resented it
blamed it even for the loneliness
it was around that time that I started to notice small imperfections
hair on her upper lip
a steady yellowing in her teeth
a contradiction in her eyes
a suggestion of receding in her once beautiful hairline
and the uglier she became the better I felt
until one day I had no more need of her
I put her in a small wooden box and nailed it shut with carpet tacks
placed her in the back of the drawer in the end of my bed
she is still in that box now
but the box is in my loft
along with my guitar and photographs of people I once knew
but I know she is there just in case I get lonely enough
in this new flat with an electric cooker and no gas

even my daydreams are damned

took a piece of pink chalk
and sketched us on a paving slab
we were dancing under the moon
it was so bloody poetic
but then out of nowhere
you told me you were seeing someone else
I hope it rains soon
and washes us both away

the day's hopeless patterns

the late shift had belonged to the idiots
each second dropping dead in front of my eyes
eight hours of bubble-gum conversation
and a head too heavy for my neck and shoulders

I missed the night bus and every inch
of the five mile walk
reinforced the day's hopeless pattern

when I got home
tired and sticky with sweat
she was in bed

her hair was as soft and long as ever
and the blanket had strayed
exposing her pale, round ass

I stripped to my shorts
got in beside her, pressed my back onto her breasts
and though this wasn't the life we had hoped for

her breath on the back of my neck
the weight of her arm across my waste
and the image of her ass as I slipped into sleep
was hope enough

make me think twice

every time I drive you to it
you pull back at the moment of impact
your heart is too big
your intentions and dreams
are too pure and strong

one of these days though
I hope you really let your strong arm go

like the time you reached up to my throat
picked me clear off the floor
all fifteen and some stone of me

but that was just too damn funny
we laughed so hard we forgot just why we were fighting

one of these days though
I hope you swing wide and clear
catch me right on the brow

I would wear that bruise with pride
and I really think you could enjoy it too

the birds were yet to start singing

I put my hand on her leg
ran my palm up her lower shin
changing direction halfway up
curving around the upper calf
the sharp little hairs
defiant after her last shave
scratched the inside of my hand
and felt like home

you don't hate me? she said
from somewhere sincere behind her wet eyes
I don't hate you, I said

the fight had not been our loudest
not by any stretch
and no inanimate objects were broken
throughout the course of things

nor had it been our longest
and we steered clear of insults
and stuck to three or four handful's
of accusations

the whites of her eyes were a saw tone of pink
she was beautiful and sad
I love you, I said

I love you, she said
she said it silently
she said it with the tilt of her head

the day had already claimed
more than its fair portion of tears
and I didn't much feel like crying

so I broke contact
rose from the couch
stood at the open window
and looked out into the night

a couple of cars and a truck
rolled by below
I liked watching the night traffic
quiet, calm and sporadic

there were no stars in the sky
and the birds were yet to start singing

I think it might rain, I said
yes, she said
we could smell it in the air

love seat

we are at that stage now, two hours into it
the stage where your ranting is a little louder
and all I can think about is how pretty you look when you get this mad
I am tired and can't remember how this one started
except that I had to work late and missed the bus
and it was raining hard, and cold and dark
and I had the usual idiots to contest with throughout the day

I remember you smiling at me, you had waited up
I remember making mint tea and burning my hand in the process
I remember letting the devil stoke the coals
I remember wanting to pull back and breathe
I remember scowling and accusing you
accusing you of what, I'm not quite sure

we are at that two-hour stage now, and I want to apologise
I know you will want to know what it is I'm sorry for
but I am tired now and all I can think about is
how pretty you are,
when you get this mad

I can tell you are almost finished
you are readying yourself for a response
but I'm tired, and you are pretty
and tonight our love seat is going to give me a crooked neck

fucking neighbours

our downstairs neighbours
hang shelves with power tools
on Sunday mornings

she smiles politely
and says hello in the hallway
he is the slight and silent type

I have never heard them fight
never a raised voice
or even a single shot of laughter blast,
through the floorboards that separate us

I did hear them fuck once
It was brief but she seemed to enjoy it

the next day I said to my wife
hey, hey, guess what?
I heard the neighbours fucking last night!

is that what that was?
she said
It didn't sound like any kind of fucking to me

big clear tear

she told me it would be okay
and even though I knew she was lying
the sentiment stuck

she told me that none of this matters
and even though that was a given
hearing her say it somehow meant
everything

she said, sometimes the heart
isn't meant to laugh

she said, often art is incomplete
it forgets its place
forgets to give voice to the
voiceless

she said, flowers and fruit
only sometimes grow
from mankind's horse shit of a heart

she told me that love was a costly debt
she didn't know if we could afford it

I watched a single tear roll down her face
it was large and clear and I saw
my reflection in it

and we sat in silence like that
for a good long while

trespassing

I'd like to wander the corridors of your mind
take off my shoes and walk on the soft floors of your
subconscious
see our surroundings as you do
search out your secrets, the ones you dare not tell me
I think I know you well enough to crack the codes
to figure out the combinations and see you as a little girl
or at least the little girl of your memories
I'd take my time, take it all in
door by door room by room
of course, the first door of interest would have my name
inscribed above it
I would open it cautiously
step inside carefully
study the layout and decor
touch and test-out the furniture
sip from the water glass atop the bedside table
pinch the black wicks of half-burnt, scented candles
pull books from shelves
leaf through photographs
soak up the scores of music
stroke the ornaments and sculptures
run fingers over your version of me
read too much into all the words, sounds and images
I'd have to stave off temptation
leave everything just as I found it
suppress the urge to tinker with your thoughts
remind myself that the slightest interference could potentially
destroy everything
come time to leave
I'd exit discreetly
already planning my next intrusion
checking my words before they're released
in case I start to blurt out something
you have never told me

her last letter

the last letter
fell to the doormat
like silence to come

the envelope was torn
and the lined paper
had a coffee ring
and red wine or blood

the blue words
transgressed the red lines
they were written by a heavy hand

they said
I cut through the park on my way home
it was raining
I watched the ducks
they are fulfilled in their fashion
I think it's because they
know nothing of happiness

my neighbour keeps chatting to me
when our paths cross on the staircase
I think he wants to be friends
I told him
friends are just
strangers without boundaries

I got drunk yesterday morning
slept through the afternoon
woke early evening with
a red-wine hangover

you mentioned a visit
in your last letter
please don't

I'd like to hand this night over

habitually walking home
because there is nowhere else to go
I light my last cigarette
and try not to step on my shadow

the evening's chit-chat lingers
bouncing around inside
like the madman's many voices

a seabird stands in the gutter
scoffing down meat and onions
from a spilt burger or kebab
he does not flinch as I pass

I give a beggar a pound coin
and resent him for not making me feel any better
he has grey-silent death in his eyes
take care, I say, as a matter of course

he says something about time travel and dark matter
but the words are lost in the orange light
and polystyrene sadness

if I could, I'd cry for this night and myself
but the tears recognise their inadequacies
and no longer flow

I'd like to take this night
and hand it over to someone who could kiss it better
of course, poetic notions of this nature
never work once they leave the page

their sadness and mine

not all the faces I saw today were sad
they just seemed that way

the older gent on the bus
with his red potato skin feet in sandals
twiddling thumbs and sighing

and the shopping cart lady
in bright white face paint
mumbling into the wind
gibberish falling from both corners of her mouth

and the sad suits
and the lonely shirts
and the brogues tapping a dreary step

today the skateboards and roller-blades seemed a little slower
two out of every three pigeons had one broken leg
or a missing foot

children filed out of the schools in an orderly fashion
as though they were cueing at the ballot box
or clocking out of a long day in an abattoir

not all the faces I saw today were grey
they just seemed that way
sure each one has their share of sadness
fair or otherwise
but for the most part it was projected
by the eyes of their beholder

it can wait

lay on your back
allow the dust of the day to settle
let tomorrow come
or not come
study the imperfections of the ceiling
let the dogs of life cock their legs and bark
let the world wait
it deserves to wait on occasion
cross your ankles
watch your round belly
rise and fall
rise and fall
most acts of urgency
are a stinging piss into defiant winds
close your eyes
and let the dreams do their work

taking back time

sitting in the park smoking a long cigar
I wondered how many trampled leaves there were
and if they were jealous of the stars

I wondered also if the foxgloves ever tire
of staring at the floor
if the willow ever felt invaded by
those seeking shade
if the less trodden grass gloated over its
yellowed and flattened counterparts

I was sitting on a wooden bench
my cigar was full in body and rich in flavour
it coloured my spit wonderfully
and I knew I would be able to taste it for the rest of the day

sometimes you meet someone

I once struck up a conversation
with an old and ugly man

he looked me directly in the navel and said
please don't talk to me, I prefer to be alone

brimming with enthusiasm I told him
I prefer my own company too!
he rolled his eyes as I continued
we are the same me and you!

he struck a match
lit his cigar stub and shuffled away
I watched him leave and wished I had a mentor

his shoulders were rounded yet light of load
he didn't smile, yet there was none of the usual sadness in his eyes

he graciously weaved through the crowd
a cushion of blue smoke around his head
he side stepped the passers
avoided the strangers

good lord, I said to myself, he is actually invisible
and with that he was gone

if I were an artist

of the type who increases the value of his paper
by soft shades of pencil and rich textures of brush stroke
I'd take a fine-line pen and draw a black and white butterfly

I'd take extra care over the wing patterns, creating them equal
as symmetrically sound as my hand would allow
but the inconsistencies and the imperfections would be
charming and almost beautiful

of course, he'd have some sadness to carry
but I'd give him a strong back and stronger legs
strong enough to leave the page in a flutter of freedom

I'd open the window nice and wide
and my black and white butterfly would circle the room
and linger a while on an outstretched finger before he made his escape
and I'd wish him luck as he flew up into a sky full of pencil-sketch seagulls

portrait

all she wanted was to be pretty
in a blue sky kind of way
she wore a dress of white
lace panties and expensive shoes
she posted her picture
on every wall she could find
until everybody knew her name
she never woke alone
and when she didn't feel pretty
she forced it
with painkillers and cocktails
she painted hazel eyes
on her eyelids and winked
and she was so very pretty
and so very sad

magnolia

I light a cigarette, place it in one of the four grooves
of the ashtray and stare at the wall
it is magnolia
the paper-sealed tobacco turns to a perfect cylinder of ash
silence falls, the world slides
becomes nothing more than magnolia
the phone rings
shocked, I shriek
pick it up and throw it at the wall
it smashes into silence
and again, all is magnolia

her shadows and mine

old skin and thin hair contradict her personality
there is so much of the little girl about her
uninvited, she sits beside me on the waiting wall

I ask how she is and in turn she asks me
I tell her I'm tired she offers sympathy but I know
that she understands tiredness better than I

so I give her a cigarette and her brown teeth celebrate
by forming a crooked smile
I gesture a light with my small box of matches
she wants to smoke it later

we have run out of things to say
we tell each other to take care
and retreat toward our own respective shadows

truth whispers

at this time of year
and at this hour
you can't hear the tree's
whisper
but by the look
of its naked limbs
and the cracks
in the concrete
above its roots
I think it is still
telling the truth

French manicure

she thought about getting a new sprinkler
for the freshly mowed lawn
he had worked on it for an hour, sweating

he was sweating now
while her pondering moved to the kitchen
where she would have him fix the dripping tap

she let out a little moan
while he worked away with his tongue
she thought about the loose floorboard
in the bathroom
the sticking back door
the shelving unit, still in flat-pack form

she tightened her legs a little
against the sides of his ears
and moaned

she looked at the top of his balding, bobbing head
and thought about the faulty ballcock
preventing a decent flush
he was flushed now and sweating

she let out a little squeal
he worked a little harder
she looked at her fingernails
he had given her vouchers
for a French manicure

she raised her legs
moaned again
squealed again
screamed a bit
and sighed

while all the time
studying her perfect
fingernails

yesterday's news

toward the end section
between a life insurance add
and a list of sex phone numbers
inside one of the cheaper tabloids
lay a slim and short article
about an older, German couple
who, during sex
fell through an open window
in the throes of passion
and in the clutches of each other
they hurtled, tits and balls in the wind
to their deaths
initially, I thought
now that's the way to go
then I considered the undignified aspects
of their demise
of their exposed and broken bodies
but then again
however we dress it up
every death is naked
brokenness mostly belongs to life
and all death comes from dying

seaside

it isn't the salt air
or the birds
or happy childish memory
of happy childish laughter

nor is it escape
a break from the city

nor a gathering of thoughts

it isn't about
peace or power

or the absurdity
of existence

or the recklessness
of a manic-depressive god

it's just about
standing on this rock
and looking out

ghost woman

I see you at the wishing well
tossing in a brown coin with
broken clicking fingers
whispering prayers I have no stake in

I remember you mostly in the abstract
from the corner of a lazy eye
you were the one I never met
and I was the one you wish you hadn't

you told me you liked the peripheral
you said, that's where I hide

I see you in long-gone conversations
about god's whim and other
worthless things

I saw you in your suicide dance
and I watched you come back to life

you used to wear that long black coat
and boots and deceit
you were an artist when it came to
brown-eyed lies

I loved you in stages
and hated you all at once

I see you in retrospect
with your brown coin at the wishing well
with silent fingers
and though they are no longer any concern of mine
I hope your prayers are realised

an under bite and additional needs

Eric had an under bite
and learning difficulties

the under bite was neither here nor there
and the learning diffs were just a category
somewhere for Eric to be placed
for the purposes of paperwork

an explanation
a label
a way of saying
you don't understand us, Eric
and we, sure as shit, don't understand you

Eric lived with his mother
her name was Claire
she was a slip of a woman
but she loved her son with a fierce might

when Eric was a baby
he fell from his mother's arms
and landed on his head
he lay on the floor
looking up
silent

Claire picked him up
kissed his little head
blew on his tiny face
vowing never to forgive herself
a promise she kept to
throughout her life

William Hill

I slid my winning slip
under the security partition

the cashier stared
his face like a rough brick
his eyes alive with contempt alone

and we stood there like that
breathing the stale air
body odour
piss
defeat

I stuffed the cash
into my inside pocket
nodded and ducked out

there were no winners

an old song

the older man
lived out his final years
in a bungalow built for two
he had two chairs
a love seat and a rocking chair

he hadn't sat on the love seat
since Marie had passed

on the hallway walls
hung many photographs
of family members captured
throughout the various stages of life
school photos
graduations
weddings
days out at the seaside
picnics
barbecues and the like

the pictures had become
a part of the walls
and he barely noticed them
as he walked from one room to another

he had a portable radio
which sat static
on the kitchen counter
in between a well-used toaster
and a largely ignored microwave

during the bleak hours
when he could not sleep
he rocked in his chair
smoking slow cigarettes

tapping ash into the tray on his lap
listening to old songs
on his old radio

like many of his generation
he had looked forward
to a long and recuperative retirement
now, in the midst of his rest
he was bored and alone

he was not much more than a boy
when he started at the chipboard factory
where he stood at a hot and noisy press
and laid veneer on would-be coffin lids
within the first forty-five minutes of each shift
his shirt was drenched with sweat
and the insides of his upper arms were red-raw with friction burns

he worked
in a shoe factory
where he steamed the leather uppers supple
and made small talk in the smoker's canteen
at tea break and lunch

he picked, packed and assembled various products
including but not limited to
toiletries
pharmaceuticals
magazines
home ware
and electrical goods
in many factories and warehouses

he had married young
had three children
two girls and one boy

he wanted the best for them and insisted on higher education
to his knowledge it had served them well

a considerable portion of time had passed
before a concerned postman raised the alarm
they found him sat in a static rocking chair
in a decomposed state
an ash tray sunken into his lap
they walked into the kitchen
and by the socket on the wall
they switched the radio off

death on a Sunday afternoon

it seems that most of them
through common human practice
are determined to solidify my suspicions

the days roll on in cruelty
with a scorpion sting of a smirk
no wonder suicide is a leading cause of death
no wonder nobody wants to talk about it

death on a Sunday afternoon
murder on a Tuesday evening
it is ours
yours and mine

whether we choose
to take ownership of it
or not

the grapefruit is not a metaphor

sometimes
in life
all things
should be boiled down
to a single moment

take the grapefruit
cut it in two
prepare the flesh
with a sharp knife
sprinkle the sugar
look at it

in that brief moment
before the first taste
there is nothing else

just a man
about to eat
a grapefruit

three little piggies

after work
on a Thursday night
outside the aquarium
three pretty girls
made up like twenty-five-quid whores

one on the floor
her legs spread
her hello kitty panties
twisted to the side
her shaved cunt open and exposed
she has puke on her chin
she's laughing and laughing and laughing

her friend is up against the wall
piss dribbling down her cocked leg
splashing and spitting and sputtering

the third is on her knees
she's trying to find her purse
she's crying, moaning and wining

there is so much hate in this city
and I'm starting to realise
only some of it is mine

war cry

I didn't know what the song meant
but I sang it, loud
because every note was a weapon
every chord a shield

I sang it loud
I sang into the face of death
I hit the drum
and sung harder

and I saw the black dot
get smaller and smaller
and the waves turned in on themselves
and the lizard lost its legs

I spat on dry dust
wrote my name in the mud
the hot sun kept it there

I sat in the devil's chair
and beat that drum
and beat that song

I defied the gods

you are a one-time deal

your roots will keep on growing
out of the bottom of the pot and into the blotting paper
those little spells of madness are okay
don't let them tell you otherwise

you know the truth about shooting stars
and that is why they hate you
their conversation is a daily punishment
don't enter into it

the box they made for you
out of intricate workmanship and rare wood
is a tightly nailed coffin
shit on it

sacrifice your fingernails
leave them in the wall
whatever it takes
just keep on climbing

their small minds are numbed
from a perpetual suckling at deceit's tit

they are threatened by you
misunderstand you
want to stifle or kill you
shit on them

don't worry too much about the chest pains
when it's time to go you will hear it coming
your type always do
and believe me, life is tougher than death

take time to breathe
share thoughts with the inanimate

focus on the largely ignored
let the moment take its time
learn from the moths and the elephants

quick and fast

sure
the world is pretty
he said
and ugly too

but we are just specks
on a meaningless rock

life is quick and short
none of this means shit

she took his hand
placed the palm
on her chest
and said

then why the hell
does it beat so hard?

bird on black water

when I could not sleep
I took to walking
there were no workers
and the air was free and light
I saw a bird on black water
I am sure the bird saw me

moths dressed as butterflies

she was artistic
and regularly cruel
as it often is
with creative types

she would present him
with a series of paintings
wrapped in brown paper

two square frames
of a seed and a flower

three box canvases
of moths dressed as butterflies

he would place them
above the bed
and during a shared cigarette
they'd stare into the paintings

when her painter's hands
were unproductive
she'd look at him and see
summed up in his pale eyes
everything sour in the world

she would let go
from the ground up
rip the paintings from the wall
destroy them in front of him
retrieve her love from him

accepting her ranting
as part of her art
he had learnt the long lesson

he pulled silently
at inner resources
watched and waited

two or three days would pass
before new brown-paper wrapped
offerings were placed
above the bed

and they would share a cigarette
underneath them
stare underneath them
and wonder how long
they would last

crueller than kids

when his father died
the other boys were
exceptionally cruel

taunting him at every turn
about his dead dad

one fat-faced kid
all cheeks and lips
and a tongue too big
for his mouth
made up a song

and they sang it
in the playground

your old man's dead
your mum ate his head
your sister put the body
in the garden shed

years later
in one of many factories
I spotted him
I saw the boy with a dead dad
only he was a man
and so was I

I switched off the
shrink-wrap machine
and walked over to
the end of the packing line

I asked him about the years
in between now and then

he told me he had been in and out
of work and in and out of hospitals
and various other institutions

he spoke with slow purpose
as though he couldn't quite trust
the words to form as he'd intended

he picked up a heavy box
and put it onto a pallet of other
identical heavy boxes

it's good here isn't it?
he said
he wasn't being sarcastic
he meant it

he told me that in hospital
he'd met a girl
who let him be her boyfriend
in fair exchange for medication

he told me this while he finished
stacking and wrapping the boxes
then he pulled the pallet with a pump-truck
into the loading bay and started all over again

I told him
I thought they'd given him
a rough time at school
I told him
kids can be so cruel

he asked if I'd kept up
with any of them
I told him, no

he continued stacking
box after box and his
sweat patches spread

I asked him if he had
kept up with any of them

he stopped working and said
no fucking way
kids can be cruel
but adults are crueller

then he went back to his work
and I went back to mine

predestination

god sits in a quiet corner
of heaven
smoking a lonely cigarette
he turns to the son
and the spirit and says,
how the hell
did it all go so wrong?

faith

if the substance
of your hope
isn't the betterment
of your lesser
then your prayer
is dust in the wind

in her letters

she'd said it'd been
a tough year
but no tougher than
the others
each month has its
measure of dead sons

she had a way with words
she knew how to sum things up
she said that poetry
is only a minor lie
she told me that we would
be forgiven
she said that sin is usually
subjective

she told me about her son
she said
he reminds me of his late father
and that makes him
hard to love

she told me about her travels
how the same stars
tell different lies
according to the sky
they hang in

I think she is an
alcoholic
her letters are sad and
sporadic
she is emotional
philosophical and a
terrible speller

I don't think of her
as mentally unstable
she just couldn't settle
her acute sense of
conscience

she said that guilt
got her out of bed
in the morning

that she felt
everything
all of the time

she told me about
her dead husband
he had three crutches
she said
he never gambled when
he was drunk
and he only ever got violent
when hungover

in her early letters
there were glimmers of hope
but hope only kisses
the lips of strangers

I haven't heard from her
in a while
I don't expect I will

some days

if it were a mystery
to be solved
then there would be
clues

if there were
an answer
then there'd be
no need for art

if it were a race
then death would
be the prize

some days are
for the taking

some are for
shitting on

the rest are
somewhere
in between

it's all lies

I hate her, she said
hate who? I said

the girl in the poem
she said

the girl in the poem
is you, I said

you bloody fool
she said
you romantic
liar
that bitch has nothing
to do with me
she's all you
you made her up
she's a man's idea
of a woman
she's no kind of
woman at all

I didn't know
what to say
she was right

so I picked up
my pen and wrote
this one down

it's all lies

it's complicated

love is the most complicated
of all of life's mysteries
that's why we are so scared of it
where as hate, like us
is simple and stupid
that's why there is so much of it
going around

tea for two

numb in the hell
of a dead marriage
she watched
from her side of the
breakfast table
as he removed
a tiny piece of egg shell
from the tip of
his tongue

he placed the shell
on the plate's edge
then forked another
mouthful of egg

she considered this
and concluded;
our life is a
weak cup of tea

how are your eggs?
she asked
good, he said, thank you

no bother
she said

then she went into
the kitchen
where she boiled water
and made a pot of tea
for two

a music theory

you say you can't read music
but that's okay
because your notes
were not made for the stave

another life, another world

one of
the factory
girls
the one with
other worlds
for eyes
used to flirt
with me
at the
production
line

but I
was young
and naïve
and my
wife to be
was
pregnant

my son
was inside
stretching her
belly
kicking
eager to scream
at the world
outside

the factory
girl
fluttered lashes
over other
worlds
but I was

young and naïve
and my
wife to be was
pregnant

always fighting

it was early and hot
I didn't feel like admitting
to my hangover
so we were yet to fight

my sunflowers were
getting ready to flower
I watered them and
settled into the couch

you cracked the window
sat in front of it
and let the breeze
brush your hair

I looked at you
I looked at your hairline
at the thin-green sunflower stalks
at the beads of sweat on your temples
and knew I deserved every accusation
knew I was unworthy

I was guilty
long before you called it

I wanted to tell you so
tell you that you'd been right
that my love was a glass of piss

but the ball of beer
and irish-cream liqueur
grew and turned in
my belly

you stared out the window

gently scratched your inner thigh
with finely kept fingernails
and I wanted to admit defeat
but I knew you'd take me at my word

I walked into the kitchen
poured a drink
seriously, you said
you're drinking already?

stop with the fucking nagging,
I growled
sat back on the couch
watched your shoulders slouch
and knew, I was wholly unworthy

confessions

it is hard to lie
especially to oneself
when all else is sleeping
every good confession
comes in the dead of night

incarcerated in canvas

I painted another picture of you
last night

and hid it with the others

it's getting to be quite a collection
it's getting to be a little weird

you are in black lace
thick fishnet thighs
your wrists are tied

you are on canvas and paper
and chipboard and ply
against a backdrop of red-brick shadows
in the lamp-lit night

we spoke at the bus stop
briefly
husky
deep
unabashed
you rolled your tongue
and told me the time

I have captured your voice
with acrylic
tonight will be charcoal

with thumbs and fingers
heal and palm
I will smooth out your rough edges
and you will rub off onto my hands

trapped inside my furniture

I painted you on the base of my drawer
you are leaning in an abandoned car park
I have made you a little more robust
which has absolutely captured your character

your stockings hang a little lower
than they ought
perhaps not to your taste
or anyone else's for that matter
but it doesn't matter
because you are covered by
socks and belts and boxers and undershirts

as one day submits to another
and various garments are removed
a little more is revealed
and I feel I'm getting to know you
beginning to understand you

sometimes I even talk to you
all complimentary of course
I'm thinking of a pastel
on the inside of the wardrobe door
a straw hat and a summer skirt
with a slit upside the right thigh

perhaps you will learn to love me
in spite of your confines
perhaps you will one day answer me
despite your confines
perhaps you will breathe a kiss at me
despite your inanimate persuasion

I am sure of my love for you
but you will never know

because I think my behaviour would
appear creepy
if I plucked up the courage
and if you were agreeable
and you came over for dinner
and stayed the night
and saw my impression of yourself
trapped inside my furniture
abstract and obscure

patti's still got it

the water under pero's bridge
was still, as was the city
during its best hour on a sunday morning

she was playing a tin whistle
you couldn't get away with calling it music
but the sounds were far from unpleasant

from my side of the river
I could see the market traders
setting up their fare, on their side

the crisp air tasted fresh
as it will when so few of us
are sucking it in and blowing it out

soon enough the crowds would arrive
and the air would become heavy
and the tongue would become numbed
by a mouthful of death

from my bench, a metal affair
cold and reassuring
I could see she'd been eying up my cigarette

she slid the whistle into her breast pocket
stood and walked with purpose

can I have a cigarette, she said
sure, I said, offering her the pouch and papers
can you roll it for me, she said
sure, I said
can you roll me five, she said
sure, I said and took to rolling

she retrieved her whistle and played
covering and uncovering the holes with her fingers
watching me roll with her eyes

her hair was the colour of wet straw
she was pale and very thin
but she carried a heavy weight
like someone who's held the truth about people

at the fifth cigarette's completion
she showed me the soft side of her hand
I lined them up on there
and she counted them out loud

one
two
three
four
five

instead of thanking me, she said
I saw patti smith in concert
oh yeah? I said, has she still got it?

she tucked her whistle and cigarettes away
put her hand all the way down the front of her jeans
held herself like that
gyrated and confirmed
patti's still got it

with that said
she returned to her original position
on pero's bridge
where she played her whistle

across the harbour
the market traders were chatting up

their first customers
I could hear a siren from somewhere distant

I stood from my bench
waved a quiet goodbye to the whistler
she lit one of her five cigarettes
and waved back

play the sad violin

there is a stranger inside
who refuses analysis
a sickness, an undefined nausea
who over the years
has formed her own personality

she is dying down there
the scent of death on her breath
is overpowering

I can hear her playing
the sad violin
the notes are in my chest
and in her eyes
she plays in A minor
a song I can't quite hear

her salty tears
coat the back of my throat
and strangle my laugh

she resents my peaceful surroundings
detests those who love me
insists I punish them
as she has been punished

she calls for me quietly
with a sad and steady bow
longs for me to join her
invites me insistently
from somewhere deep in the intestines

I hate the love I have for her
I should kill her
but how do you murder

an already dead flower

I could swallow poison
and silence her
but deeper down
and deeper yet
I know that is what she wants

she imagines us as dancing ghosts
far from all the others
embraced in a smokey waltz
our bare feet
light and free
on floorboards of dreams and mist

but the other woman
won't let me go
she doesn't hide her song from me
and you may know something of love down there
but you know nothing of her

her tears stand out in the rain
and though she is cynical of the promise
she believes in every rainbow
she washes my face and wants me to live

she tells me to look after myself
she looks at me expectantly
trusting we will reap as we sow

she does not play the sad violin
yet I hear her song clearly
as the oak
as its limbs
withstanding strong winds

she places her head on my chest

straining her ears to hear
she wants to get to know her
but I won't let her
and neither will she
we are too jealous for that

and it is breaking all of our hearts

dead stars

he told her
to look at the stars
at night and think
of him looking at them also
but she couldn't settle the sadness inside
or help but think about the stars in their sight
being far gone and out of reach

saddest song in the world

sat down on a hard chair
guitar on knee
fingers poised

I said
I'm going to write
the saddest song in the world

she turned her attention
toward me and said

sweetheart, you've already
done that
a number of times over
maybe it's time to try
something else

as if everything were okay

they made it all look so easy
idle chit chatting
talking small

as if everything were okay

as though the ground didn't pull
as though the sky didn't push down

they must have been given the answer
or perhaps they never thought to question
either way, they made it all look so easy

sinister tree

in spite
of the deafening
second-hand clock
time seems a little
slower tonight
there are no stars in
the sky
and the sinister tree
across the street
sings a loud and fearless
song

goodnight

better
a
night
of
restless
contemplation
than
a
peaceful
sleep
on
a
bed
of
lies

when we were kids

growing up in a small market town
we didn't have a shopping centre
or a cinema, or a train station

the police station had two cells
the library had three sections
the museum had a penny farthing

my brother and I used to sneak
behind the slaughter house
and lift the lid of a metal skip
so we could look at the animal innards
and the maggots therein

the stench was phenomenal
I can smell it now

our school was white
and other than the healing
held all the aesthetic qualities
of an old hospital building

during long summer nights
after longer blue skies
of the type which only exist in memory
we would climb onto the roof
and smoke our secret cigarettes

one of my teachers
hanged himself
as did a boy
a year my junior

all of this was
before the age of

mobile phones

my friends and I
would make prank calls
and laugh inside of a red
telephone box

I stepped inside of one the other day
for old times sake

there was a fine black spider in there
hanging from the receiver
he looked like he'd been there for
quite some time

I dialled a number
and while I waited for an answer
I thought about suicide
and rooftops
blue skies and cigarettes
maggots and animal insides

early grave

he worked himself
into an early grave

his family never wanted
for much

because he worked himself
into an early grave

as the crow flies

some say
only trust yourself

as the crow flies
I am seventeen years
away from you

I didn't trust you then
and I don't trust you now

time and space

toward the end
his requirements were simple
he looked forward to Tuesday evenings
when she would catch a bus
to her weekly book club
and he would slice up a grapefruit
pour sugar on it
eat it with his fingers
in front of the window
where he would watch the people
and their dogs and the rooftops
and the rain
she had found the spot on the bus
where the vibrations were just right
her journey was well practiced
and she could time her pleasures
a few seconds before her stop
when she came home
he seemed to her, more tolerant
and she seemed to him, more tolerable
she spouted some literary guff
and they would linger a little longer
when they leant into
a goodnight kiss

dead hope

looking for god in man
is an idiot's errand
hope dies in the hands of men

at the end of their rainbow
sits a colour blind guru
who has lost the little wisdom he had
to a crack pipe and a hip flask

his scraggly beard is stained by tobacco juice
his staccato prophecies are obscene and irrelevant
he is shrouded by an acrid stench of disappointment
has an unequalled relish for public masturbation

he is a two-way mirror projecting and reflecting failure
all the failings in those who seek him out and his own

he speaks to the truth seeker from the corner of his toothless mouth
in pointless riddles that make no sense
but the journey has been too long and the sacrifices are irretrievable

on account of dead hope being too severe a dose of bereavement
most set their legs as the lotus and strain to believe

doppelganger

if I had a doppelganger
I'd use him as a scapegoat
the anger turned in would all come out
I'd keep him in a soundproofed storage unit
I'd blindfold and gag him
and all the thoughts I shouldn't have
would take aim and manifest themselves
in unspeakable acts of cruelty

my mannequin and I

we watched tv on the love seat together
the bottle seemed to go down smooth and fast
but I don't think she touched a drop

she is the silent type
doesn't laugh too much
and keeps her cards close to her chest

I ordered in but she wasn't hungry
she was grateful of my large appetite
I don't think she approves of waste

I purchased a nice floral number from the charity shop
it hung a little loose on her hips but she was glad of the
gesture all the same
she likes to take things slow
that's okay with me, I too am a little prudish

I told her about my mother
I told her about my plans for the summer
I told her about a lot of things, she is such a fine listener
I'd like to get to know her better
I think she is pretty beautiful

I pecked her on the cheek goodnight;
perhaps a little forward
put her in her cupboard room and
dreamt about our future

drunk on your tears

like cracked and split grit
your piece of wood and strings
sing from somewhere beneath
the bruises

you are showing anyone who'll listen
what it means
to lay the soul naked

you pick and pull at stitches
with crotchets and quavers
you brand the flesh with a red-hot
treble clef

please stop playing
your blood-heart music
I can not take it
you're stripping everything away

the woman who allowed him love

he'd wanted to say
a few words at the ceremony
but there were none
he looked at their faces
their clothes
their lives
he saw them as one
collective disease
unaware
graceless
dead to the art of breathing
and he realised
without her
he was just another part
of them
she was like a glass thorn
razor sharp and transparent
she stared at the night
pointed a finger
at dead stars
and called them
cunts
she said they were
false prophets
she was all woman
strong
complicated
beautiful
the ground had been stolen
from underneath
she was gone
and there was nowhere to fall

fade away

she is a burnt out matchstick
bruised by thought battles
lost in the war of herself

I picture her being saved
by myself or anybody else

taken to a safe place
where there are
clean towels and avocados

she could lock the bathroom door
stand naked under hot water
all soap and steam and skin

but she holds her own hand
and she doesn't want to be saved

I guess I am soft, overly romantic
I ought to mind my own affairs
and let her fade away

he left his soul on the floor

the bird stepped from the wire
and fell like a dead burden of feathers
the man watched and thought, suicide

moments before impact the bird
spread its wings and took flight
disappearing into a dreary sky

his fellow pedestrians
a mass of swinging bags and barging shoulders
had not noticed the bird

he stepped into the road
at a pace wholly at odds
with the angry traffic
but the drivers only acknowledged him
as an incomplete thought

past the far side of the street
at the foot of the food market's hill
there was a chalk sketch of a seaside love scene
on a pavement slab

beside the drawing sat
a tip jar
an open can of Special Brew
a tin of coloured chalk sticks
and the artist

the man
from two backward paces
saw something in the picture
and he couldn't stop looking at it

he couldn't see the chalked lover's faces

but he could see they were happy
they were headed towards the sea
which the artist had created, warm and inviting

her hair and his open shirt
waved and flapped in the summer breeze
they were comfortable in each other's secrets
his fingertips were tucked into the waist of her shorts
resting there, on her furthest hip

they knew how to fuck
how to make love
how to fight
how to fall and breathe

the man stood there like that, staring
he thought about love and loneliness
he thought about the city and suicidal birds
he wondered about happiness and the
romance of the coast

he named the pair
he called them Errol and Claire
and he knew what it meant
to hear your name spoken by the voice
of the one you love

he knew that Errol and Claire
had a hidden place on the beach
where Errol had kissed Claire's inner thighs
pulled down her shorts
taken in her warmth, her scent, her taste

take me, Errol
she had said,
take me,
and he did

the artist shook his tip jar
I've poured my soul onto the floor, he said
are you going to grin at it like an idiot
or are you going to pay for it?

the man put a ten pound note
and a five pound note in the jar
which, excluding spare change
was exactly half of what he had to his name

the artist picked up his tin of chalk
and his can of Special Brew
and hurried away with his earnings
he left his soul on the floor

Acknowledgements

The author would like to thank the following publications where some of these poems originally appeared: Rusty Truck. The Idiom. Least Bittern Books. Prolific Press. Hobo Camp Review. Vending Machine Press. The Round Up Zine. Vagabond City. Literary Orphans. She's In Prison. Walking Is Still Honest. In Between Hangovers. Kleft Jaw.

About the Author

Matthew J. Hall's poetry and short fiction has been widely published in various magazines, anthologies and online literary ventures. He reviews small press books for The Small Press Book Review and at www.screamingwithbrevity.com. His poetry chapbook, Pigeons and Peace Doves was published in 2015 by Blood Pudding Press. He currently resides in Bristol, England.

Better Than God
Peter Jelen

Euthanasia is a firing squad, the Catholic Church brings the Son of Man back to life with the Shroud of Turin, doctors create imaginary mental disorders to further their careers, and God hands in his letter of resignation in the form of a suicide note while lonely young girls seek out pedophiles on the Internet just for some attention.

Better Than God is a collection of dark and humorous fast-paced imaginative stories filled with unforgettable characters only Peter Jelen can provide.

Better Than God
$12.99
6" x 9"
254 pages
ISBN-13: 978-0988075016
ISBN-10: 0988075016
BISAC: Fiction / Short Stories

Knuckle Sandwiches
Wayne F. Burke

Knuckle Sandwiches is a punch in the face to art, culture, and society. A smack in the mouth to propriety. Knuckle sandwiches of the literal kind as well as the more common, but no less painful, metaphorical kind, which life gives to everyone regardless of race, creed, class, or gender.

Knuckle Sandwiches
$14.98
5.25" x 8"
116 pages
ISBN-13: 978-1926449081
ISBN-10: 1926449088
BISAC: Poetry / General

garbageflower
Damon Ferrell Marbut

With garbageflower, Damon Ferrell Marbut demonstrates once again how each book is its own unique expression of human engagement. The generosity of this collection comes from the shared moment, wherein often Marbut leaves defining the poem's purpose up to the reader. Other times there is no doubting how firmly he believes there is no line separating abstraction from reality. This believable, touching book of poems is for everyone.

garbageflower
$15.00
5.5 x 8.5
102 pages
ISBN-13: 978-1926449074
ISBN-10: 192644907X
BISAC: Poetry / General

Heaven's Gone To Hell
Andrew J. Simpson

Heaven's Gone To Hell leads the reader through a series of humorous dystopias that challenge the way we use language and the way we see the world. From alcoholic archangels, to heaven's reliance on unpaid labour, to a devil just trying to do what's right, Andrew J. Simpson's follow-up to The Big Picture turns the tropes of society on their ears.

"The mind of Andrew J. Simpson is an ideas machine … His brain is actually a powerful alien computer."
~ *Alejandro Bustos, Apartment 613*

Heaven's Gone To Hell
$19.99
6" x 9"
174 pages
ISBN-13: 978-1926449067
ISBN-10: 1926449061
BISAC: Fiction/ General

Remote Life
Edward Anki

Remote Life slices into the reader's mind like a paper cut, provoking thought, mild discomfort, and the unsettling thrill of a direct and immediate experience of reality. In this collection of poems, Edward Anki addresses the disconnectedness of modern urban existence in raw and unforgiving terms, offering an unfiltered take on everything from the struggles of dating to the stark actualities of aging and death.

Remote Life
$10.00
5.25" x 8"
46 pages
ISBN-13: 978-1926449029
ISBN-10: 1926449029
BISAC: Poetry / General

Impressions Of An Expatriate: China
Peter Jelen

Impressions Of An Expatriate is an honest, firsthand examination of one expat's experiences living in China dealing with culture shock, racism, and assimilation. From his encounters with children grown in cages to bears fighting to the death in a pit at the base of the Great Wall, Jelen's poems leave little to the imagination with haunting, vivid portraits that will take you on a trip.

"Jelen observes everything going on all around him, and as he sees it happening, he's taking it in, and becoming wise in the ways of the world…"

~ *Carl Miller Daniels*

Impressions Of An Expatriate: China
$8.50
5.25" x 8"5
60 pages
ISBN-13: 978-0992035563
ISBN-10: 0992035562
BISAC: Poetry / General

Hearing Voices
The BareBack Anthology

Since 2012 BareBack has sought to publish writers who are straightforward, sincere, and passionate. Hearing Voices: The BareBack Anthology features the most innovative and honest poetry, fiction, and flash fiction that has appeared in BareBackMagazine since its inception. Hearing Voices is bold, brave, and a great showcase of some amazingly talented new and established writers from around the world.

Hearing Voices: The BareBack Anthology
$14.99
6" x 9"
132 pages
ISBN-13: 978-0992035549
ISBN-10: 0992035546
BISAC: Poetry / General

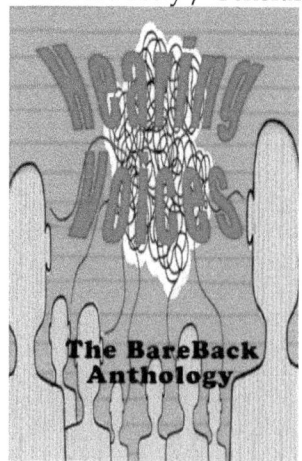

And So On...
The BareBack Anthology

A collection of innovative poetry from poets speckled around the world who have been featured in BareBack Magazine ~ an online publication dedicated to BareBack writers. People who aren't afraid to take off their gloves and give the world sincere, unpretentious, honest writing that has punch. *And So On...* is dark, humorous, and sometimes downright strange.

And So On...: The BareBack Anthology
$17.99
5.25" x 8"
134 pages
ISBN-13: 978-192-644-910-4
ISBN-10: 192-644-910-X
BISAC: Poetry / General

Be Kind to Strangers
Carl Miller Daniels

A wild and wondrous group of poems, BE KIND TO STRANGERS is the most recent collection of work by Carl Miller Daniels. Sweet, sexy, and alarming, with more than a hint of gentle absurdism, these poems cross the paths from sadness to joy, with a sense of awe and amazement that things in this world, are like they are.

Be Kind to Strangers
$8.50
5.25" x 8"
56 pages
ISBN-13: 978-1926449043
ISBN-10: 1926449045
BISAC: Poetry / General

DICKHEAD
Wayne F. Burke

One of the best volumes of poetry published this year or any year, DICKHEAD is an absurdist knuckle sandwich that deals in realism and farce in equal measures: simultaneously a punch to the gut and massage--jasmine mixed with hemlock--a ride through the Tunnel of Love and into the Fun House...An eclectic stew of poetry that engages both soul and spleen, heart as well as mind.

Dickhead
$13.00
5.25" x 8"
108 pages
ISBN-13: 978-1926449050
ISBN-10: 1926449053
BISAC: Poetry / General

ALSO BY MATTHEW J. HALL

PIGEONS AND PEACE DOVES

www.barebackpress.com
Hamilton, Canada

www.ingramcontent.com/pod-product-compliance
Lightning Source LLC
Chambersburg PA
CBHW060158050426
42446CB00013B/2893